Cool Women
Volume Three

Cool Women Volume Three

Eloise Bruce
Carolyn Foote Edelmann
Lois Marie Harrod
Betty Lies
Joyce Greenberg Lott
Judy Michaels
Penelope Scambly Schott

COOL WOMEN PRESS
Rocky Hill, New Jersey

Published by COOL WOMEN PRESS
5 Toth Avenue
Rocky Hill, New Jersey 08553

Cover: Picasso

Library of Congress Cataloguing-in-Publication Data
    Bruce, Eloise
    Edelmann, Carolyn Foote
    Harrod, Lois Marie
    Lies, Betty
    Lott, Joyce Greenberg
    Michaels, Judy
    Schott, Penelope Scambly
    Cool Women Volume Three

ISBN 0-9707812-2-9
    1. Title
    2. Women's Studies
    3. Love poetry
    4. Poetry

Library of Congress Number 2004114608

To the cool men in our lives
and
in memory of Gary Lott

Cool Women Talk Woman Talk

Cool Women in the Landscape

Cool Women Sing the Body Electric

Cool Women
Talk Woman Talk

Penelope Scambly Schott

Practicing

All across America, the widows
sleep with their radios on,
    the sonorous announcers
    speaking only to them,

and my mother, who has never
been cold, is always cold,
    until the sky finally lightens
    as the widows plan lunches,

as they phone married children
to come sleep in the guest bed
    which is always ready
    with fresh sheets.

After each visit, the widows
empty the wicker baskets,
    not sniffing the sticky wads
    of Kleenex, knowing

that the kind man on the radio
will murmur all night,
    holding them close
    with the gentlest music

until a huge sun erupts
out of the black woods,
    and the sky
    unfurls so fast that from my side

of our rumpled bed, I practice
returning to girlhood
    where I slept alone
    with the Lone Ranger.

Turn up the old radio. Punch
down the quilt. Pound hard
    at the stuck
    door of the heart.

Who is that masked man
always coming toward me?
    Who is that man
    riding away?

I've Always Loved

I've always loved the
men who must be wooed,

the king who didn't have to talk:
riding under a small-grained moon,

all colors of the snowy road
curved in to fit his waist,

the Horse King with three eyes:
he called me Rose. Little Swallow.

Iris. Ash. The Least One.
In his mouth I knew the name was mine.

Asleep under a quilt of tulip petals
feathered like the wings of birds,

the grain of something imperceptible
gashed the instep of my foot,

to this day I wear the scar,
although I never point to it.

A small room hung with carpets,
swirl of leaves left in the cup,

my future was laid out
–mirrors, shreds of fabric,

the king of iron water:
he told me I was salable,

foot washing, towel, basin.
I longed to run away.

Two times I've drowned,
I know the undertow,

the loss of vertical,
head hitting bottom.

Perhaps my instinct
was the right one after all:

I had already drowned
and who could say I wouldn't drown again

looking for the king
of hell-for-leather,

foaming and stamping in his stall,
too hot for me to handle.

Her Comma-Shaped Nostrils Like Hot Balloons
after Picasso

They hadn't fed the damn house for months
but now she didn't want to leave it empty.

For god's sake, he said. *It's not starving.*
Toss the carrots into the disposal and let's go.

Non, she said lightly, throwing a French word
back into the closet they could never fill.

Absolument non—just because we've always
starved it doesn't mean we must starve it now.

He thought again how inserting French
in an English sentence requires an acrobatic mouth.

But she was already tearing the boxes:
pie pans, rolling pin, measuring cups, spoon.

At the kitchen counter she sifted the flour.
She rolled out the crumbly crust.

Outside he was revving the motor
in his third language. *Toujours les mots.*

Damnit, she would make an apple pie before she left.
Defying gravity, her tears fell and rose.

Joyce Greenberg Lott

All Those Hammered Nails

Late Friday, you needed a shave.
I used to rub against Daddy
after work.
Nails, rows of hammered nails.

But the story you told–
years ago
about poking in mother's drawer.
Under her bras?
You didn't say.
Did she wear girdles
with garters
that pressed like pink lips
against blue-veined thighs?
Mine did.
No matter. Your story wasn't about underwear.
You were sneaking around
mother's drawers,
found her diary,
read it.
With sweating hands?
You didn't say.
Mine are wet now
writing it
but after all,
it was your mother. No matter.
You read her diary,
that's what counts,
I can hardly believe it,

8

she was a secretary
put the good parts in shorthand.

You were a man
even then, sixteen, seventeen?
Was there black hair
on your chest?
No matter.

Men never learn shorthand
so you never learned about your mother,
like I'll never learn about you
and all those hammered nails.

Judy Michaels

Season's Greeting

In this tinselled waiting room
to is fro. Heat and motion, alive
in bone and brain, shimmer *attract*
repel, like holidays we're not sure
how to observe.
I can't help noting how the menorah's
plastic, smooth-tipped flames in reds
and pinks look more like lipsticks—
a rack of Persian Melon, Crimson Frost, Blood
Wine. My platelets dropped too low, I can't
have treatment. This is called "chemo holiday."
Time off for bad behavior? Time on
to celebrate disease? I could bleed
too easily, the cat needs his claws trimmed.

Let's all dream of knife blades under water.
Slowly their gleam draws us down
to mark the old year's passing.

Let dreamcells drown
in bubbly. Welcome the daily
yeastiness of mind that can
face both ways at once.

Carolyn Foote Edelmann

Olympia's Cat

her black maid stands
inscrutable, cradling
his variegated bouquet
staring blandly at the one
presuming to venture
toward Olympia's sanctum
once again...

but she remains serene
thoroughly in command
five fingers curl along
that rosy available thigh
only her gaze snapping
with the cat
dark as the silken riband
circling that haughty
wounded throat

the cat is NOT pleased!
every inch of fur electrified
expression livid
thin black tail abuzz
above that Gothic arch
of back

if he dared to touch those whiskers
they would all ignite

Eloise Bruce

My Dalmatian Reads *archy and mehitabel*
"expression is the need of my soul,"
archy

i'm a dog in this life, not an old soul. channeling
cleopatra's cat, who still dreams of asps and eye-
shadow, not eels and ibis, she whispered my first life as
an illiterate musician in the 36th colored infantry.
killed by a blow to the head by robert e. lee's horse's
front hooves, she sighed and giggles about it still. the
jiggling of it makes my head itch. there are the ghosts
that tickle my feet to wake me until i speak in her cat
voice and she reads my mind and finds mehitabel a
charming figment. howling, i discover that my next life
was as a vers-libre poet and that is why ghosts cling to
my fur. i cannot write with my paws and sometimes
stand up-wind of the poem and catch it in my nose and
sign it wallace stevens with wags of my tail. my last life
was as a snake and before that a frog and that a
butterfly, because frogs eat butterflies and so on.
in the happenstance of the universe, i was supposed to be a
hog but i mistakenly came back as a dog who has the
appetite of a hog. i am an american soul, an american
man won't eat an american dog and i am hoping to
become a river in my next life. this business of ghosts is
full up with quirks and uncertainty.

12

This Rose is for You

I give you the tips of the thorns
in the pads of your cow-handed fingers,
I give you the sparse sap
for your guzzling mouth,
I give you the tight green petals
that circle the rose hip,
I give you the faithful man in the rose garden
plying his clippers and rake,
I give you the tin bucket
where slit stems drown.

If ever you gave me a rose,
I don't remember it;
if you promised tomorrow,
I don't remember that either.
I don't even recall why I loved you.
If you cast more than a small shadow
in a cut field at the height of noon,
I didn't see it.

I remember grasping the wing of a gray moth,
I remember the powder that stuck on my two fingers,
I remember how much it tasted of nothing.

Eurydice's Version

Every girl dreams about a man like that,
not handsome merely, all-around,
an athlete, stars in his own band–
the whole town's hero, might be half a god,

aloof–then, just one look at you
and he's a goner! Suddenly you've got
his letter sweater or his ring,
you stand to watch him, glowing in his light,

and everybody hangs on him,
they worship him, your dog,
your grandmother, your friends
would die to take your place.

What's more, this man adores you
to the point of madness, there is nothing
he won't do for you. He'd
go through hell for you.

And still, somehow it all ends up
his story, a tale of skill and daring,
what he did for you
and how he did it,

what he saw and what he said.
At last it hardly matters
how you came to be
among the shades,

you limp out when you're called
to take your place and track
his shadow through the dark.
Then he turns around.

This is the part your mother
never told you, nobody seemed to know.
It's not all perfect,
being loved so much.

Dear Mrs. Dalloway

I look in yellowed envelopes
with thirteen-cent stamps,
ones I eagerly tore open.

I've lost something,
the photograph where I was smiling
with straight teeth.

Snow wasn't falling
on more snow.

I search pages
with filled-in commas,
faded vowels
where typewriter ribbon wore out.

I buy paperwhite bulbs,
plant them in rocks,
anticipate spring, but smell odor
trapped in my rooms.

No one told me
how the past grows inside
like a tumor,
shrinks the future.

How a fist can't close
around memory,
how everything changes
when we're not looking.

I want to have a birthday party
without candles.
I don't want to blow anything out.

The Punch Line

And the preacher said, "shut your damn mouth, woman,
that's fish you see." At a Saturday night supper
somewhere in my childhood I heard my first joke.

Daddy, I haven't seen you in twenty-five years,
imagine my surprise at receiving your letter:

> "Eloise, have you accepted Jesus as your savior?
> Remember, sins don't send you to Hell;
> NOT believing does."

First Man and First Woman left the underworld.
They came to the earth through a hollow reed.
They found a girl child.
She gave them the land between four mountains
and four rivers. The people rose from her skin.
When she rubbed her right armpit
the Bitterwater Clan was born.

The joke goes like this:
A woman is being baptized in a lake.
After the first dunk, she cries out,
"Jesus! I see Jesus."
Then the preacher says the part about the fish.

He wrote, "Hell is full of good people.
But, if you believe that Jesus died on the cross
for you and me and he will come again
to take us to Heaven, you are saved.
Please favor me with a reply."

How can the punch line be "shut your damn mouth,
    woman"?
From Angel Peak the girl child watches the Glittering
    World,
Monster Slayer, Child Born of Water, and Beauty
in the House of Dawn.

Lois Marie Harrod

Bread

Sometimes the past returns,
as a student whose knees
seemed too narrow to bear

his classmates' jeers,
queer, faggot,
his voice so foreign

you astonish yourself
when you call out his name,
Michael, and it is.

He's traded his thin white arms
for a leather jacket and shoulders
broad enough to hang a sleeve,

a soldier now, holding
the sky above Somalia,
an ebony bowl in his hands.

His friends have told him
to write the stench of Mogadishu,
he has friends now,

but he wants to tell you
about the white stars rising above the desert,
and as he looks at your ceiling,

the lights seem to float
like a basket of bread in the evening.
Thus he begins singing his songs,

this boy whom you do not remember
saying a word in your class, his voice
now a white loaf in the sand,

and all around, the students
roll up their eyes from their dry study
as if they too were hungry,

and you wonder what crust
you could have thrown him
that made him come back to you today.

Spring Outburst

On tiptoe to sniff lilac–
two wings and a heart
burst out of the bush.
Rhythm of God, this Sunday radio's
phrase for a jazz sermon, call
and response, though you
don't see the shrub's on fire with
flight when you thrust into its
purple business.
                Rhythms of God,
when a cell sparks and booms, renewing
last spring's tumor, miniature Nagasaki,
the cloud opened like a fiery flower
and birds came tumbling down.

Not simple as inhale
exhale, body of spring you're
born with. A bomb's tucked up
inside your head.
If it doesn't call, why do you answer?
The mind's intent, hungry
for patterns, for heartbeat.
Will the lilac
explode this time? Opaque
its purple script, and the bird
already gone.

Confidences

once my Mother told me
things no child should know

I still see her yard:
weathered pickets/windfall apples
the empty picnic table
light battling through dry leaves
of our old climbing tree

Mother's words came frothing
in unwelcome freshets
fetid stream that tunneled
underground for decades
tunnels to this day

spills across the rocky
hammer/anvil/stirrup
to my brain
no dam shield

Mother has not spoken so again.
of course, my sister claims
I made it up

Flying East for my Grandson's Birth

And I'm sailing in high silver over Pendleton and Bozeman
as you journey the last hard inches toward the sill of the
    pubis.
Talking centimeters.

At 33,000 feet, the outside temperature, according to the
    screen
and these frost flowers blooming here on the window by
    my seat,
is minus 59 degrees Fahrenheit.

Council Bluffs and the rectangular plains marking buffalo
    bones
in late snow. Now the thick Mississippi twists like an
    umbilical,
and the cord, coiled through generations, tightens my groin.

Push, they told me, and what else could I do, my back
    cracking
over the rim of the world?

                            At the darkening edge of the
    continent,
she is breathing and sweating. Let somebody's cool hand
sweep damp hair from her forehead.

As I pass over Cincinnati, she is opening in waves and
    scarlet
birth blood is flowing through us all. East now of
    Pittsburgh,

she is riding her moment of *I can't do this any more,* the
    body
almost inverting itself, and clouds rushing under my wings,
until the lift and gasp in the moving air.

Sometimes we call this
landing.

Child, I will tell you every glorious thing I know:
We are made out of dirt and water. Someday your hands
will have freckles and lines. Many cherished people
have lived and died before you.

Oh, and, child, one thing more:
this earth invents us and consorts with us willingly
only because we tell stories.

Joyce Greenberg Lott

Living in a House without Men

Within, a long table. In the center,
a bowl of green apples,
unafraid to be bitten.

Upstairs, you'll find a tub
filled with warm water
and a mermaid singing as she bathes.

You will marvel at the light
over every workspace,
and at the gray-haired woman

dreaming about the bird swaying
on the branch outside her window,
never losing its balance.

The Mother's Confession

Your heart doesn't trouble me so much
as what I find in mine.

That spring you were born, so cool
the colors ran together, magnolia into lilac,
white pear, weeping cherry,
the world spread out for us
a sea of bloom.

Perhaps it's just those days we hold
against each other: that we were almost one,
but failed. Now it shames you
that you sucked my breasts, I held you
naked in my hands and washed you everywhere,
knew secret things no one should have to
give up to another.

Once, when you cried endlessly,
I dived so deep into my panic
I understood that I could throw you at the wall
just for a moment's quiet. After that
I never trusted tenderness.

There's nothing I can do
that doesn't start a storm, ragged
and whipped by wind.

I've worn transparent
as the sail of some old mariner
come back to tell you things
you do not want to hear.

This water's bitter. Arctic cold.
The burn of salt.

Carolyn Foote Edelmann

Upon Reading Eloise Bruce's *Rattle*

If were a storm god
I'd tend our entire planet
because of this cluster of words
and the small clutch
of rare Golden Club
soon to lift its forest
of arms like gilded sparklers
above teak waters
below that pale dam
that holds back yet creates
the shimmering lake,
as form compresses and releases
her poems

I must read *Rattle*
out loud
to drown out sleet,
wishing each gelid barrage
did not feel like nails
heard from within
my funereal box

Judy Michaels

Amtrak: Baltimore to Trenton

The Quiet Car is in the front—it is
Quiet, we have dimmed the lights
and there are signs
not to use your cell phone.
Business Car at the rear—
which is where I am,
doing my business not so
quietly, mind outraged,
screaming *shut up*
to itself, my phone won't
turn off and besides, there's no
footrest. How the hell can I
conduct my business, which is
recurring cancer, without
a footrest? I paid for it, dammit,
the abdominal incision's raw,
aches for what any suit on an
expense account wants–security,
a little extra support over abominable
bumps in the old, eroding
bed of rails. It hurts to bend,
it hurts not to be quiet, but quiet
is at the front, miles of lurching cars
ahead. And I have baggage.
Mind winks–chemo, *you mean*
you have chemo, and questions, and
you're too short, your feet don't reach
the floor, you need a footrest

and the Quiet Car that's up front
quietly pulling us north through a night
of sirens and cell phones and maybe
a suicide on the tracks, quietly
dimming our minds so we stop
receiving signals, we don't even
read the posted signs, each of us
becoming our own car, trusting—
and this sounds crazy—that quiet
will take us where we have to go.

Bathing Jack

1

If you die of this stupid disease,
I'll toast you, slinging my full glass
in your face. You told me I could enjoy it too.
I promise to drop *HOWL*
down your bare spine
one word at a time,
wash you in mothers' milk.

2

Before you got sick, Peter found the bear pit
but gave it to you. You took the curious there
to see the rotting cows left as bait.
You loved the notion of hunters baiting bears
and used it to seduce all comers.

As freaky as you,
the end of a double rainbow
plunged into the meadow.
Bathed in its irony
you jogged through its arch
returning from the bear pit,
a sweating stranger in tow.

3

It's raining buckets;
not rum, semen, or urine
blood, spit, or gasoline,
but cold mountain water,
in the smiling photograph, you
barbecuing back of the lodge
after the sky opened up.

Any minute you could drown
in the tears of your lovers.

Lois Marie Harrod

Yoke

And what did I hope for when I hoped, immortality?
That gold coin passed from one hand to the next

then suddenly lost in a drawer, closet, chink, dropped
so that an earthquake later, volcano, hurricane,

it can rise to the surface where gold has no value
or small. When I was thirteen, I hoped fairy tales,

the fish on the table cleaved open, and lying there,
the endless life in its gut. I am a princess, I am a beggar.

When I was 15, I memorized Thanatopsis
while I was ironing my father's shirts

because my Latin teacher said everyone should know that
       hope
by heart: So live that when thy summons

comes, you will be starching your father's collars.
Didn't the old book say something like that?

It is always been my hope to cram more things
than possible into the possible, the collar first, the stays, the
       yoke,

the cuffs, the sleeves, this is how it is done, first things first,
the bed, the lip, the mouth, the rising up, the lying down.

Cool Women
in the Landscape

My Altitude

Female, born not far above sea level
from the small sea of Momma's womb,
I cannot tell where the tide ends and my blood begins.
My heart does not have the muscle
of mountain people, and my skin longs
for moisture. I could slip back into the water in a single
    beat.
Most things come to rest on my altitude
or roll, fall, or stride through it, wheels, bullets,
and bombs and our bodies at rest. The relics of saints are
    here,
and sap and rivers run their course.
This is the place where small shiny wings hum,
and there is the rustle of things that scurry.

Judy Michaels

Walking at Low Tide before Breakfast

Here at the edge of the saltwet
is a place for losing mothers
again and again.
Women our age walk barefoot here,
shoes dangle from one hand, the other free
to scoop up shells, stones,
any striated thing
whose lines the ebbing tide has licked
bright and clean.

Here silence is dizzying
close-up, like the backward pull
of pebbles underfoot.
                    The women's eyes
lose themselves for a time, then lift,
heavy-grained with sleep, to search
for distance. Today the rim of the sea
is mist-bound, even the nearest
islands gone, their shapes,
their trees, cedar, sequoia, visible
in the mind still, like voices
of late mothers in the night
singing notes that refuse
melody, each note dropped
separate as stone,
I am a word
that means gone.

Back on Route 212

This trip, she thinks, has been
a slow flaying, skinning back
the layers of her life
until she's peeled to something
pink and unreliable:

the city where she fell in love
flooded and grey,
the friend from college beautiful
but slightly crazed,
her high school classmates
caught by a warped lens
that turns them old, or else
almost unchanged, the first boyfriend
still slender and ironic.
Front doors
she can't go up to, and the lake
so full it seems to drown itself,
but on the playground her Big Rock,
her hand still knows the holes
that once held some historic plaque,
fallen before her birth.

Now to see her mother.

Nearing Glencoe, she comes up even
with the freight train she's been chasing—
caboose, coal cars, box cars, tankers—

long flexible sinew of the prairie.
Two engines—no, four.
When it sounds its whistle,
she can taste yesterday like salt.

Penelope Scambly Schott

Up in the Wallowas

The mountain goat at three days old
stood on his mother's back;

he lifted his new white face
over five mountains and the house of wind.

Because it was dawn,
snow shone pink on the east slope,

and the blue glacier ground in its bowl
a thick milk of rock.

Down at the base of the mountain
cars went shopping in long lines.

A lenticular cloud hooked on the peak.
Time formed at my feet. All morning

I stood on my mother's back
as if I were wise to be born.

Carolyn Foote Edelmann

Visitation

I finally reach
a windy crest
my turquoise jacket
welcome against
spring's late chill

I feel more than see
the eagle settle
upon flat granite
to my right
he gulps that entire landscape
at one glance

slow, steady,
I extend
my arm
so he can step determinedly
onto my padded sleeve

my eyes are not one inch
from his
so gold, flickering
flames surrounding the dark centers
as coronas ring an eclipse
gaze steadier
than any
I have ever known

gusts ruffle
his dark shoulder feathers

42

stirring blue glints in sun
the air could not be more electric
if he were bearing
thunderbolts

he rests his left cheek
against my own

inside my heart
small fists tattoo
within that rosy cage
some prisoner
implores escape
wakens me
to life without eagles

The Nature of Clouds

There is a cloud on my house.

The cloud has arrived in strings and wisps and ringlets. The cloud has wrapped my house away from thevalley. When I step outside my house, the cloud is on me.

I stand outside my house in a place like rain. The rain moves neither up nor down, just very delicately toward the east.

What color is the cloud? Pink and opalescent gray. Maybe if I were outside the cloud, it would be black.

What does the cloud taste like? Rhododendron. Pink star rhododendron lifting spiky petals into the gray.

What does the cloud think? Hill. The cloud thinks about leaving this hill. The cloud misses the western ocean. Nobody has told the cloud that when it comes to the snowy mountains, it will break. The cloud doesn't fully know the nature of clouds.

When I open my front door, pieces of cloud waft into the house. The pieces float among sofas and chairs.

Now the cloud is stuck inside my house, and I am sad for the cloud. Therefore I open the back door to let it move on.

The rest of the cloud streams through my house. It touches

papers with its moist breathing. It swipes against walls and makes them shine.

My old dog lifts her head. She watches the cloud go out the door. Then she puts her muzzle down on her crossed paws and thinks the thoughts of a cloud.

Neither the dog nor the cloud will say what they are thinking. Maybe they are lucky and think only in wisps.

A wisp is coming to me now:

> *I am ten years old on the summer lawn and my father, who is still blond and gawky, is doing a somersault on the sweet grass. He has huge black shoes.*

My father has gone to where the cloud is going, all broken into molecules, and where my old dog will go soon.

When I am dying, I will try to remember the day there was a cloud in my house.

I will wait like that cloud for someone to open a door.

Maine Landscape

A porch rail peels outside the window
where my husband sits painting a watercolor.
He's taken out our table and covered it
with his orange and yellow beach towel,
so I won't see paint when we eat together.

Two butterflies hover over the larkspur
he is putting into the foreground of his picture.
I watch them suck, each its own blossom,
and then dance in the air together.
"Look, they're mating," I say out the window.
"How do you know?" he answers.

A single pine, with awkward limbs, stares back at me.
I look past its loneliness to yellow grass
(Hopper grass, my husband says) and then
 to the sea. I'd swim to that island,
the one just beyond the sailboat, if I could.

But the wonder of this moment is
I don't want to do anything
or to have anyone do anything for me–
paint a porch rail, catch a butterfly, cut grass.
I just want to sit by the window and watch

the shadows my husband's arms make
on the orange and yellow towel
or look up at the cloud that floats like a white roof
or a soft steeple over the island,
beyond the sailboat.

Lois Marie Harrod

Figure in Tree at Sunset

You can see that the tree is thorny, matted, leafless
branches like tangled clumps of hair but you cannot
tell whether the figure caught in the fusty web is

male or female, whether he or she is looking back
at you on a slower ridge or is looking at the sunset,
that sky streaked with cheap crimson. This is so

often the way with meditations on trees at sunset,
figures appear you cannot quite flesh, flatlanders,
calculations on whether you will die of the same

grief your father is dying of, looking backwards into
the night, or from the grief of your mother who watched
the sun drop like a lozenge into the mouth of the sky–

the acrylic cough drop a beginner would wreak
on a page with too much orange and too much
cadmium yellow. Yet dabblers do draft

bits of earth to convince you briefly that someone
is walking with you in a garden as old as a song,
the sort your father sings until he is hoarse

and sneezing at the nursing home where he will never
be happy again. And how is he grieving but as
the figure in the tree? Which way is he facing but both

ways–the Janus of all those spats that filled their
hours, where was the cat, what would they eat for
dinner, he never liked rice, he wouldn't eat biscuits,

47

she's still complaining. He must have turned away from you, he must be listening to her speak, he must be weeping as you wish you could weep.

The incandescence

under white clusters of cactus spines, the slag
end of another heartless day, where sundogs
on the sparse clouds double the heat over desert
tracks and pale husks of stalks I can't name,
pods and rattles slicing my bare shins,
and my skin the skin of a parched toad recalling
a cold rain on the porch floor you dragged
your bags across that day you left. Where now
is the grocery sack spilling your boots or the jeweled
buckle of a tooled leather belt beating the steps
as you went? That was hard music you sang me,
not love songs, not crickets, never farewell.

Chamber Concert

And then it happened, when I didn't expect it–
water falling like stars.
I heard it in the restaurant
before the concert
(almost didn't recognize its sound).
I hadn't even reached the door
when I smelled it.

As we listened to the chamber music–
the dark velvet sounds of Smetana
mourning his five-year-old daughter–
we heard the cello spill
with the sweetness of summer rain
that had waited and waited to fall.

I had forgotten how parched
my limbs and tongue could be,
how I need to bathe
in something besides sunlight.

And then I heard the cello sing
like a stream that had waited and waited
to flow, the full-blown grief of a father
who had tasted the oneness of God.

Jazz Sister

Okay, I understand about the groove:
the pluck, the pedal, the hush hush whisper of skins,
the thud flick flick thud regular as morning
coffee–after all, we grew up with the same
mother, tuna casserole every week–and those
left-hand chords that keep to themselves,
pretend they don't know what the hell your right
hand is thinking.

And I kind of get the scales, too arbitrary if you were
in at Creation and heard all the pitches flying free as a mad
      cat,
but still, music needs syntax to jazz with,
though we poets like the blue notes best.

What throws me, what makes me wonder how you
got some gene I missed out on so you marinate
salmon in maple syrup and make it
taste good–what mystifies me is
the hummingbird stuff,
that improv.

You do this in public?

It's Double Dutch. I never figured out
how to jump into those two ropes crossing
while both ears were being sawed in half by
lamebrain chants about don't forget the red hot
pepper.

I have to go off to some rock at the end of the world
and get my poems before dawn, so even the sun
can't watch.

But you just walk on stage and arc and dive down into the
     lily's
throat, or hover, invisible beat of wings on the blue edge
of time, a tease, a meditation, a chromatic fall
into sugar, cupping silence with a syncopation.

It's courage music, that says anything is
possible, fluke, flinch, sharp, flat,
slow dance up the mountain–
maples to birch to pine, deep woods
or a sudden clearing.
You're one cool traveller on the sylvan way,
playing the light and shadow as they fall.

At Hopper's Gas Station

Poised against the darkening,
there's Pegasus midair, the red pumps
sentinel, round heads alert and bright.
A man, his back to dusk,
arranges things in expectation.
Somebody's moving this way
sure as gathering night, as gradual.

And there we are, just down the road
around the curve of evening:
the four of us, in our old grey Model A,
rear-window curtain drawn,
a death's head for the gear shift knob.
Two cranky in the back,
two in the front weary of squabbling.

The little station's light is cold,
thrown against the road. What can it offer
tattered travelers? What sustenance
to knit us up? Dry sandwiches and
bitter coffee, cabins out in back
with saggy double beds
where we would get no rest.

No, we won't look for comfort here:
we'll stay together, stay
inside the car, drive on. Maybe
if we keep at it long enough
we'll punch through to the flip side
of the canvas, where a sizzle of sun
is just about to dazzle with its rising.

Relations

Twenty-five years ago my great-uncle and aunt
lived on this lake with cows and blackberry bushes,
all gone to scruffy woods now, ablaze this fall
as John Michael and Patsy spread Daddy's ashes
off the dam. We all feast on turnip greens, catfish
and hush puppies in the home place turned

restaurant, sipping ice tea, the fried food turns
my husband's Yankee stomach. My aunt
Marjorie sits opposite, delicate with her filet of fish,
my father's steely hair on her head and bushy
eyebrows above her dark eyes, and Granny's ashen
circles beneath. I am the sin-eater and we are fallen.

I am surprised they have chosen me to take the fall;
the bad first child of the first wife took her turn
to read T. S. Eliot and not the Bible. Ashes to ashes
recites the able second wife's child, Suzy. My aunt
has stopped directly addressing me. Perky and bushy-
tailed Suzy charms and I am a flapping fish

out of water. She abundant as Jesus' loaves and fishes
and actually speaking in parables. My face fallen,
I could flop into the cool under a nearby bush
lie in the dirt and think of the turn, turn, turn
of this and all seasons in the verse my aunt
reads, then rise restored from the dark and ashes

like Cinderella or a phoenix out of my own ashes.
Jesus said to the apostles, I will make you fishers

of men. I am drowning in my own blood, the aunt
and the cousins. They might, any minute, fall
to their knees and pray, all heads upward, turned
to heaven and me still looking for a burning bush

to guide me out of the wilderness of this ambush.
I push through the undergrowth, to find the ashes
of my father floating in the lake. Grief will turn
to winter, spring, summer and another fall.
We all become dust one day, food for the fishes
or the worms, some sooner than others. My aunt

will return to God to join my father who loved to fish.
He caught bushels before his gray bone and ash
scattered this fall, untouched by our last blood aunt.

Post-Mortems

the first shark–the huge one–
I vanquished, though it tore
at pristine flesh

the next group I battered
with my hand-made, hand-held
tools, managing to take a few
with me

but it was the third round–
those that came by night
those beyond counting–
ripping, sawing, tearing till the seas
ran red, studded like mosaics
with the bright white flesh

that final onslaught conquered
–leaving only backbone
and the well formed
tail–floating among the detritus
ashore

Tourists In Cefalu

Below the looming skull of stone, sea breaks,
three shades of blue, and we've been dazed

by a cathedral's dome, that gold mosaic
Christ, so cool, inclusive, arms embracing all

of Sicily's invaders, with his blond Norman hair
and Arabic black beard, his Byzantine long nose.

Back in the square, under a broad umbrella,
we sip our dark espresso. A sudden motion:

crowns and crowns of funeral flowers
rivaling the sun, and then a coffin

carried in procession from the church. The priest
in black, a line of mourners: widow walking, bent,

the family weeping; at the rear, joking and gossip.
You rise as they pass by our table: your eyes

brighten with tears, and I am thinking
that my single indrawn breath diminishes

what breath is left to me, but you are thinking
of the man himself, nailed in a box, never

to sweat under the sun, to feel again
his knuckles scraping rock, the salt sting

at his hands as he hauls in the net,
silver with leaping fish.

Judy Michaels

February Night

There had been a lot of chaos, pages of fast black notes,
        or maybe it was just this night wind
                rattling the oaks that hold
our hill and house where I lay reading
        Borges's lost lectures on the riddle of poetry,
                end of a long week marked by
the black trumpeter, beaten by police in Madrid
        who mistook him for a thief,
                he kept entering the lost riddle, playing
                        a slow drag,
till my afghan's crocheted colors grew warm and swirled
        me into
                sleep, where skies were clearing and you
                        lifted your hands for the downbeat,
we both were on double bass, our arms
        strong and curved and tender around
                the music, over there four other
bassists bowed and swayed, we were new
        constellations, everywhere joyous
                recognitions as flutes found other
flutes companioned with a horn or drum,
        and so we played and waved
                until we knew something was over–until
we had filled the room with blue-green
        trees and a blur of hills,
                or at least, when I asked you to show me
a conductor's score, you laughed
        and opened an endless scroll
                of blue-green hills.

Lois Marie Harrod

"Landscape laid open like an old newspaper"
James Wright, "Drone and Ostinato"

And so we've read this before, the goldenrods
gone gray, wooly as yesterday's lambs, I can't remember
what I said to you a year ago. Perhaps we were talking
of the neighbor's child who did not live. Weather

intervenes, the sun mutes the choke of news,
this is all that is left of the blue jay's rancor,
a few blue feathers. I have always thought such truths
deserve such deaths, the way they sass, they jeer,

but today, I allow their tricks and brash,
the way we do, reading day-old papers, knowing the out-
        come,
self-indulgent and prophetic, all those words

that someone spilt like ink, all that light and brass
over the next hill, an open hand, an old path, a lost glove
that the dog picks up in her mouth and then discards.

Carolyn Foote Edelmann

By Lamplight

I would return to the caves
carry a small flicker of light
in the pointed clay lamp
that just fits
in the palm of my left hand, leaving
the right free to fumble
and to know the true

contours of this mammoth's haunch
quick swelling of auroch's chest
smooth hollow at the bison's sooty flank
the cave itself collaborating
in new art

Eloise Bruce

Cages and Doors

It rains a lot here and the expanses
of glass glisten, never enough light
to see clearly. The sniper's car
often passes slowly. It is carved up
like a tin can. I wonder why
the police haven't noticed. Jesus,
the roof is flapping in the breeze.
I am wired

       for metaphor, sleeping or not.

I am in the foyer of my
unconsciousness, too large to keep clean
with rooms that redecorate themselves

so often that I can conjugate
the metaphor. I am the house,
she is the house, we are the house.

My first husband inhabits my current husband
who, some nights, demands a divorce. He is my father
by the time he closes the front door behind him.
New doors appear willy nilly, making it impossible

to find the aviary to prevent the birds from starving.
Doors, and birds and there are cages

and singing and starving. Sometimes
I don't remember the birds exist. I am Alice

and he is Rip Van Winkle, and you are too.
They are Alice and Rip, and we are too.
When we sleep, the metaphors play
croquette and ninepins. When we wake
we are young or old or young and old.
You are young and I am old.
She is young, he is old, and we are the metaphor.
Do not turn on the lights, find the doorknob.

Joyce Greenberg Lott

On Winter Days

When the snowplow's not been out
and old oaks, draped in white,
know everyone shoveling their driveway,
I wonder where birds hide,
red-headed woodpecker, chickadees
who fluttered at feeders in darkening sky.
We hide, too—my husband and I—
behind spices and soups,
apples saucing on stove, forgetting
tasks we spent days accomplishing,
checkbook tallies and grocery lists,
lesson plans to improve others' lives.

For now, I contemplate white blankets
laid to rest on roofs. Suppose
that the sun will never come out,
that gray-white light is all I'll ever see.
(At ninety Mother's almost blind.)
So brave, I think, or foolish,
all of us who never give up,
who spend such energy
changing the landscape of things.
Why not accept
this neighborhood covered in snow,
wait like birds, precarious in winter oaks?

Lois Marie Harrod

In the Very Distant Universe,
Objects Older than Light
headline, *The New York Times,* 1/14/2000

I try to imagine an object
farther than light,

a stony owl
beyond the moon,

all the dark matter of my life,
rash and wreck–

how much the black rhino eats
to save himself

and yet every black hole
recedes from him–

bone that precedes skin
and devours it,

the place where the hardwood chair
moved across the deep,

the black rose emptying
the firmament.

A child hits his head
and sees red dwarves

but he can't remember
their heavy feet

and what can I make
that anyone will keep?

An infant with the wrinkled face
of her grandmother?

I believe a skull inside a stone
differs from a skull inside the vase

but I have only one hand
and its dark art

and I want to count the black hair
in the white cat's throat,

every feathery paw
that sprawls the sparrow.

I do not remember
the first time I was kissed.

Someone is walking in the snow
like a crow.

Cool Women
Sing
the Body Electric

Viva

The past is a book of empty pages,
nobody ever really lived in it.
Try to imagine Verdi and his Giuseppina
at their mustard-yellow villa in Busseto,
lying dark, sated with sex,
sniffing the strange perfume
coming off each other's music,
townspeople scribbling Viva Verdi
on the walls, or Shakespeare
about to brush the dust of Stratford off his jerkin,
screwing Anne in the next-best bed
as toads and bugs thunk from the thatch,
downstairs the old folks nodding
around the ingle.
    Picture your parents
licking chocolate off each other, or
heaven forbid, your mother's fragrant sigh
as you start waiting in the wings
to make your entrance
on the stage of instantly-the-past.
You'll play a short love scene,
recite some lines, forget the rest, go off.
When did the moon get full again,
spilling its cup of borrowed light
as if that petty glare could clarify,
illuminate, convince you anything
was ever real?
    None of it happened,
all of it is happening, it's done with mirrors,
strings of them, wavy and fogged,

reflecting everything at once,
the nothing that is there.
And even as you're writing new scripts
with the sharp pencil of now
a big white gum eraser follows close behind
and the moon struts its pocky show
against the seamy backdrop of black space.

Lois Marie Harrod

Foxgloves

So many entries into the body, the five fingers,
the senses, the thousand delicate caves
of foxy pleasure, and then the follicles, the pocks,
my 89-year-old mother after her hip replacement,
the pores on her neck like craters, dry tunnels

for thick needles, and then her anger's sting
as I tried to keep her from tearing out the IV poked
into and taped to her forearm, tried to keep her
from tearing out the catheter. It pinched, she said,
it burned, how did they expect her to pee

with that stuck in. God doesn't want us to be manipulated,
she said, a word I had never heard her use,
this woman with a fifth-grade education who had
always left theology up to my father, this woman
who had been a shy and docile wife, now snippy

and witty under the lingering influence of anesthesia.
She wanted to go home, what would Dad say? Dad
died, I said gently, you must stay. *Shit*, she said.
Damn, words I did not know she knew,
words that had entered her ears when she was small,

prick buzzing in her head for decades, *hell* poking
and prying, *fuck* sticking around waiting for an exit,
I didn't ask for this operation, she said.
When did you go over to the nurses' side?
What did those doctors say to suck you in?

She tried to get out of bed, she tried to go home until
the nurses in their gloves brought restraints.
They were violet gloves, she said, violet and foxglove blue.
I just want to die, she said. It was you, not me
who wanted me to have this operation, it was you.

Judy Michaels

Semi-anesthetized upon a Table:
Fishing for the Traveling Catheter

Needle-witted, the mind, pierced
with what if's, piercing, won't lie back
on the neutral pillow. It's never liked
Cross that bridge when we have to.
It spans now to never,
spins thread fine as a single
nerve that wants to stay out till dark,
play hide and seek with words.
                          It's got me
craning my neck to watch
the blood, the wire, the hook,
to ask, You do this often?

                    No.
It's rare an implant breaks off
and heads for the heart like this.
Arrhythmia. . .always possible.
Prick, push, threading an artery,
bridge of bloody thread, cross
stitch, lines for a sampler,
name and dates.

            They've fished
up my groin for hours now,
where are we going? Groin's
numbed, groin, deepthroat word,
threshold to sex, birth, groin
the connector, Groin the hero.
            More valium? Oh,

just a splash. Bonehead here
wants to stay sharp. . . cross bridge,
name names, keep track of
the coffee spoons.

Carolyn Foote Edelmann

Vultures and Blossoms

I examine the body
splayed upon wet grass
two stern vultures
swoop from east, from west
to open its chest cavity

surgical, precise,
they treat layers
of skin, of muscle tissue
like pages of a book

their straight slit
and curved lifting
are startlingly clear
as I strain to see the heart

–that fruit grove
every tree in flower
sky a pink mosaic

Swimmer

To swim among lilies whose slick stems
entangle the thighs of the swimmer
in beads of light–

a pond of yellow stars, and beyond cupped
fingers, a watery sky that trembles
into wrinkled glass.

I meant to learn to breathe under pondwater
instead of being forced ashore
among weeds,

their golden heads so freighted with seed.
Who guessed a waxen lily pad
possessed sharp edges?

Instead I am watching my old dog sleep,
shallow breaths stirring the white
underhair of her chest.

I meant to memorize my constellations,
to tell one romping Brandenburg
concerto from another.

In the month of August, certain lilies bloom
an astonishing pink, much as when
the inner flesh

of a white-haired woman, unlike the slit
of an old bitch dog, will ripple again
with quick zest.

Strawberry Ripe

They ripen on their way to market,
so when I was a girl I was taught to pick
too soon, to pluck them pink
as my virgin nipples, and as firm,

but now I've schooled myself to wait
until they're ready, bursting red—

Is anything this red? I mean
this perfect early-season-ripening red,
this lush and rich too deep for finger-cut-blood red,
for end-of-summer-setting-sun red,
red of roses, even fully blown.

It's summer's warming sign, this red,
strawberry red, this incubating red
like inner blood, like woman's blood,
this fertile red, this promissory red—

till now all of creation spreads around me
like a treasure trove, enticing me to search
beneath its canopy of green and find out riches,
sweet and red and ripe, and fill my bowl,
and fill my greedy mouth.

Atlantic City

I never asked to be some man's dream, some blonde
in a swimsuit, walking down a runway,
waving at crowds.

Fifty years later,
I drive back
through pine barrens
to a place that has changed
as much as the splintery boards of the walk I used to strut.

The glitter young girls sprinkle on their faces now
blew in the air back then,
and I swept Danny off his feet
by the length of my legs.
I was a mermaid without a tail.
When I grew scales, I swam away,
leaving Danny to imagine my voice
calling like a siren's.

I rehearse what I'm going to say–
something real after all these years,
like "Once I licked your leather jacket."

But Danny, Mr. Organizer of this high school reunion,
acts as friendly as ever.
When we introduce spouses
I want to shout, "This isn't who I am, either,"
until I feel his eyes on me.

"Grow up," I start to whisper, but instead
I rise, iridescent,
weightless as foam,
from the depths of another sea.

Isabel

She hit his life like a hurricane
that was continually downgraded–
first with the promise of a Grade 5 typhoon
that would shatter every window in his house,
and since he was a careful man and so much in love,
he spent hours taping his windows,
nailing up plywood and writing signs
on railroad bridges and dempsey dumpsters,
Izzy, I love you, and filling the rusty spaces
with sprayed-on hearts and kisses. He would stay
he told his friends, where he could greet her,
didn't she deserve it? And hadn't he laid in the beer and
    chips
and made his hottest chili?

But by the time she arrived
she was no more than a tropical storm
twirling an acorn or two in her skirts
and dropping a few branches and socks here and there.
Yes, she'd have a glass of water
maybe a coke, but she wasn't hungry,
she was just worn thin, what woman wouldn't be
with all that whirling and trouncing
at the center of her being.
And what did he expect her to do
with the whip and chains?

Later he told his friends he was disappointed,
he had expected devastation.

Judy Michaels

In Remission

She feels swollen, touches her belly
not like a woman with child
who's moon-ripe, riding
high and sure.
                    She has never known
such making. This is no caress,
she wants to push, press, beat down,
knead out
                    the white tumescence.

Huge in the desert air, a moon
leaps at her, bloated omen
of something her fingers fear
to palpate, mystery buried
deep as a fetus.

Is it a witchy power
to raise again what was cut,
burned, drugged?
She has no seeds, no pouches,
her prayers run backwards gabbling towards
child, now I lay me, if I should die
before I wake,
                    her prayers are fingers
addressing flesh resistant, secretive, already
hard and green.
                    They said three years.
Is the moon come round so soon?

Artifice

I reach for your hand across the table.
Your fingers stiffen.
You don't have time.

The rain imperceptibly wets the streets.

I wish it were storming.
I wish we could battle.

If I could undress you in the kitchen
In front of the children
I would

But I rinse the cups.

You are kind and considerate.
I am lonely.
You are shy and dignified.

I want you to cut your flesh open
Because you need me inside.

You leave for your appointment.

Order is the artifice
That frames our lives.

Yup, by cracky, this is a good old-fashioned love poem

This man asleep under my quilts, how
shall I name him? Shall I say: you are the deep
bark of a pine tree, the three-legged stool
in the dim barn, a cool slide of denim over pink
silk, or the smell of ashes and fresh soap?

Tonight you're the oak floor of the depot, a bench
where I watch the public clock; the 12 and the 6
on the face of the clock, the low hiss of the steam
locomotive slowing at the platform, the metal clang
of the conductor's stool, the gold braid on his cap,
its shiny brim my final stop but one.

Yes, I know you, monkey heart that thumps
in my belly; shall I name you *Eric*, or just the worn
wooden spoon that beats up the froth in my bowl?

The Heart

was invited
to a masquerade ball

come alone
or bring a guest

the invitation written
in a cruel script

little knives to cross the *t*'s
adolescent stars to stab the *i*'s

the heart wanted to go
but he had not learned

whom to take
what to wear

maybe the satin jumpsuit
with white sequins

but surely Elvis
would be there

and Cleopatra
with her love-sick winds

go as a lace handkerchief
he told himself

wave until
you're damp with tears

he thought
of the lovers

he had once seen rush
into the train lavatory

they came back
laughing and sighing

all the jiggling
sent them through the roof

better wear something safe
than snug

he chose black leather
and took his dog

Carolyn Foote Edelmann

Magdalen

loving you, I see
Christ must have made love
to Mary Magdalen

of course!–He was here to become
fully human
through tumultuous, impossible months
I have been shown and shown
nothing is more human
than passion

especially when everything on earth is shouting
THOU SHALT NOT

they had to be mad for each other!
leaving her must have been His gravest
sacrifice

who but a lover
washes Someone's feet
with her hair?

Dolce
for Anne and Dave

Always a song being sung
somewhere is the world, the trembling
traveling like a great underground river,
a spring, filling the mouth
of the next singer. The melody
of a wedding comes as no surprise.
This ritual and the sound of the dead
guardians, come to bear witness,
the rustling as they land
to roost in the old trees.
Their wings form perfect hearts
to shield us momentarily
from the world's troubles.

Thoughts might be rising
like the sliver of a new moon,
the glow as luminescent
as this marriage of our friends.

She may be thinking of cake,
a pink one with a slice missing.
His dreams seem to grow out
of his head like a great tree,
each dream blossoming
and bearing a tender sweet fruit.

Some one of us is first to think
of the power of two. When
this bride and groom finally
break the silence, the song
of weddings comes as no surprise.

Her note joined by his note
joined by your note, joined by mine
multiplying by ones and twos,
rushing to rejoin that great river,
dive back into the warm earth
and journey on to the next moment,
when this song will spring
from the next open mouth.

Joyce Greenberg Lott

A Country You've Never Visited

His full lips, his smooth body
open you

As though opening were simple
to even the suggestion of his touch

A stream widening into a river
river sliding into sea

You don't know his language
nor the dangers

of trespassing
in his territory

All you know is the way he dances
inside you, the giddiness

of your breath
after not traveling for so many years

Carolyn Foote Edelmann

Horse Sense

I am a stallion still
confined in winter's barn
straining against stained woods
my dark hooves relentless
against the trammeled straw

see how my veins knot and thrust
beneath a lustre of skin

observe how my eyes
color of Ohio's buckeyes
swell and glisten
despite gloom

watch the white plumes
of my furious breath
spurting in morning air

out there–even though it's April–
barely a bud
reddens the empty woods

even so, I must
burst from this stall

Ghostkill

"He thought you died last summer,"
she tells me, hand over the receiver,
and I know she wonders–is it safe

to laugh? She wants me tough,
wit-cracking, flicking ash at destiny.
So here's to death in the air, death

by wire, like flowers–dead a year
on an invisible someone's
breath. It doesn't feel the same

as being present at your own funeral,
which never appealed to me. No,
hearing you've died feels more like

one of those ghost squares in the family
album, where four black, gummed corners
went dry and released the snapshot

of you in a highchair or a wedding veil:
Where did it go? Like a phone voice
that doesn't know the listener's hung up.

Eloise Bruce

Since She Died

I notate the grief in hollows of my body
where music comes from.

In finally summer, the thousand leaves
chatter on a magnolia tree.

Enough of any small moving thing
will make a sound, just as the monarch's

wings sing while they flutter
off the trees of their Mexican home.

If enough spiders gathered,
could we hear them spin silk?

One drop of rain falls,
the storm is deafening. No one heard

the last rattle of her lungs. Not I
who lived in her and know the melody

of her blood.

The Long Heart of October

This year's fall has been like sex, the best sex,
like the sex your mother didn't tell about, or if she did
you didn't listen, mortified that she could say such things,

could know about the sweet slow building
to the brink, each day glowing deeper till you ache
with longing never to arrive, but keep on coming.

My mother has been old for thirty years,
dropping her leaves gently one by one. I meet her
at the entrance to the forest, say her name over

like a lover. Mother. Tell me what I need to know:
what I should watch for, watch out for. This time
I swear I won't be so embarrassed I can't hear you.

Fear as the white pith

I sucked two lemons under a full moon,
each tipped like the aureole of a nipple.

The squeezed juice of the lemon
stung all the cuts on my fingers.

I gave my daughter a dimpled lemon,
I gave my daughter my yellow heart.

Ripe lemons hung heavy as testicles
until the lemon tree dipped into the river

and all her cowardice was washed away.
In my next life I will worship turnips,

depth of a hard winter,
heartstring into the earth.

Speaking in Tongues

Gaze up from the street to see the cockatiels,
parakeets and parrots in my front window.
Birds are what remain of dinosaurs.

Behind my eyes more roost,
countless as barbs of the feathers
covering the thousands of hatchlings.

Waddling over their broken shells
blue jays, blue-footed boobies,
hummingbirds and all the rest

try to escape my grasp. I reach
and pluck up whichever is nearest.
I clutch them to my chest.

They wriggle and get away, some
in fledgling flight, others escaping
to the past, in the time before flowers.

Their bones are hollow, their beaks
sharp. It is hard not to crush them
and they draw blood on my hands.

Their song is deafening, the language
ancient and strange. They sing
of Sappho, and the ones whose names

they no longer remember. Their voices
are lyres, singing of how hard it is
to hold even one word in my mouth.

Acknowledgements

"A Country You've Never Visited." Joyce Greenberg Lott. *U.S. 1 Worksheets*

"Bread." Lois Marie Harrod. *Earth's Daughters.*

"By Lamplight." Carolyn Foote Edelmann. *U.S. 1 Worksheets*

Chamber Concert." Joyce Greenberg Lott. *Dear Mrs. Dalloway* (Finishing Line Press 2004).

"Dear Mrs. Dalloway." Joyce Greenberg Lott. *Dear Mrs. Dalloway* (Finishing Line Press 2004).

"Figure in Tree at Sunset." Lois Marie Harrod. *Freshwater.*

"Foxgloves." Lois Marie Harrod. *Poet Lore.*

"The Heart." Lois Marie Harrod. *Zone 3.*

"Her Comma Shaped Nostrils Like Hot Balloons." Lois Marie Harrod. *Blueline.*

"Horse Sense." Carolyn Foote Edelmann. *Edison Literary Review.*

"'Landscape laid open like an old newspaper.'" Lois Marie Harrod. *Weber Studies.*

"Main Landscape." Joyce Greenberg Lott. *Dear Mrs. Dalloway* (Finishing Line Press 2004).

"On Winter Days." Joyce Greenberg Lott. *Dear Mrs. Dalloway* (Finishing Line Press 2004).

"Yoke. " Lois Marie Harrod. *PMS PoemMemoirStory.*

Cool Women is a critique group that meets once a month to provide support and criticism for the members' poetry. All of the women have published extensively in a wide variety of journals and books.

Eloise Bruce is a poet in the schools for the New Jersey State Council on the Arts. She teaches creative writing at the Middlesex School for the Arts and was 2004 Resident staff at the Frost Place Festival of Poetry in Franconia, New Hampshire. Eloise's first book of poetry, *Rattle*, was published in early March by CavanKerry Press. She is a 1998 recipient of a poetry fellowship from the New Jersey State Council on the Arts.

Carolyn Foote Edelmann was the first member of the Princeton community accepted into Princeton University's Creative Writing Program. Carolyn photographs and writes on nature/travel/history for *U.S. 1 Newspaper*, *The Packet Publications*, and *Jersey Sierran* and *New Jersey Countryside* magazines. Her chapbook, *Gatherings*, was launched aboard the QEII. *Between the Dark and the Daylight. . .* won the 1996 i.e. press Prize. Professionally, Carolyn arranges publicity-focused events for creative people.

Lois Marie Harrod won a 2003 fellowship, her third, from the New Jersey State Council on the Arts for her poetry. Her sixth book of poetry, *Spelling the World Backwards* (2000), was published by Palanquin Press, University of South Carolina Aiken, which also published her chapbook *This Is a Story You Already Know* (1999) and her book *Part of the Deeper Sea* (1997). Her poems have appeared in many journals among them *American Poetry Review, Blueline, Bombay Gin, The Connecticut Review, Faultline, The Carolina Quarterly, Prairie Schooner, Zone 3.* Her earlier publications include the books *Every Twinge a Verdict* (Belle Mead Press 1987), *Crazy Alice* (Belle Mead Press 1991) and a chapbook *Green Snake Riding* (New Spirit Pres, 1994).

Betty Bonham Lies is a poet in the schools for the New Jersey State Council on the Arts, and a Geraldine R. Dodge poet. She is the author of four books, including a book for creative writing teachers, The Poet's Pen, and Earth's Daughters: Stories of Women in Classical Mythology. She was named a NJSCA Distinguished Teaching Artist and received the Governor's Award in Arts Education. She was awarded a fellowship in poetry from NJSCA in 1995.

Joyce Greenberg Lott's essays, poems, and stories have appeared in *Journal of NJ Poets, Kalliope, Ms. Magazine, The Paterson Literary Review, The Times, The Writer's Chronicle, Writing on the Edge*, and other journals. She won third prize in the Allen Ginsberg Poetry Awards and was a finalist for the Ragdale Foundation's Frances Shaw Fellowship. She is the author of *A Teacher's Stories, Reflections on High School Writers* and a contributer to the anthology, *Proposing on the Brooklyn Bridge: Poems about Marriage.* Her chapbook *Dear Mrs. Dalloway* was published in July, 2004, by Finishing Line Press.

Judy Michaels is artist-in-residence at Princeton Day School, where she also coordinates an interdisciplinary program in arts education. She is a Geraldine R. Dodge poet. She is the author of two books on teaching adolescents: *Risking Intensity and Dancing with Words,* and a book of poems, *The Forest of Wild Hands.* She received a poetry fellowship from the New Jersey State Council on the Arts in 1995, and in 1997 first prize for poetry in the John Harms Center for the Arts competition.

Penelope Scambly Schott is severely bicoastal. After receiving four fellowships from the New Jersey State Council on the Arts, she moved to Portland, Oregon, but remains an active and commuting member of the Cool Women of New Jersey. She is the author of the novel *A Little Ignorance*; a collection of poetry called *The Perfect Mother*; a book-length narrative poem *Penelope: The Story of the Half-ScalpedWoman,* the true tale of an early New Jersey settler; and *The Pest Maiden: A Story of Lobotomy,* as well as four chapbooks, most recently *Almost Learning to Live in This World.*